To: Miss Linda,

I'm honored to have you in my life. You've been an inspiration in more ways than you know. I love you and the spirit & humor you continue to show even through rough times. Your children, grandchildren have such grace among them. I thank you for all the love and support you've given me.

Love,
Patrice Watley-Hill

Perseverance From the Heart

Poetic Mind Vibes

by

Patrice Watley-Hall

authorHOUSE

1663 LIBERTY DRIVE, SUITE 200
BLOOMINGTON, INDIANA 47403
(800) 839-8640
www.authorhouse.com

First published by AuthorHouse 08/09/04

ISBN: 1-4184-6906-8 (sc)

Printed in the United States of America
Bloomington, Indiana

This book is printed on acid-free paper.

Art work provided by Erica Williamson

REFLECTIONS & SPECIAL THANKS:

To God Almighty for allowing me to dream and be creative.

To my children Bobby & Akieria Hall for keeping me on my toes. You are the true loves of my life.

To my mother, Maxine Watley-Rowe for giving birth to me and instilling values and morals of life.

To my father, Willie Dozier, who has not played a major roll in my life, but not to his dismay. I know I am deeply loved.

To my uncle, Oscar Watley and my cousin Oscar (Dayvon) for just loving me for the person that I am.

To my Attorney Tonya Mitchell-Graham who makes sure things are in order.

To Eboni Johnson who is also a poet, for her encouragement and unique style.

To O'keefer Thompson for taking the time to read and proof each and every one of my poems, even when he did not really have the time. For promising to purchase my book even though he has read them all.

To Sekou Lennon for your support and assistance when ever I needed. You were a good sport at all times. Thanks for pushing me when I didn't feel I had any energy left.

To Valerie Watson-Baxter for listening to my ideas and giving great encouragement to go farther, For simply being a friend.

To Diana Tuttle for her support and contributions. It's really uplifting when someone is interested in what you are doing and want to see you achieve your goals.

To Angela Stephens, Christy Vaughn, Michelle Staley, Linda Brown & Jenniffer Smothers for their critiquing contributions and encouragement. Thank you for listening when I was excited and going on and on about my different accomplishments in poetry.

To my other family, friends and coworkers who were also encouragement's and enjoyed reading some of my poetry.

Thanks to poetry.com & blackatlanta.com for the exposure.

To Dez Billingslea Producer/CEO and Urban Blu Funk/Jazz Group for giving me the opportunity to have my poetic vibes put into song. Their first album entitled "Out of the Blu" was released May 2003. They are currently in the studio recording their second album to be released late summer 2004 where I will be a featured writer on a few of the songs. This album is slated to take the group to a different musical jazz plato.

And last but not least I would like to especially thank Author House for their expertise in book publishing and to J.R. Harris, you are the greatest. Without your help and patience I would have been lost.

DEDICATION

To my grandmothers Fostine Watley, Hattie Dozier and my aunt Earnestine Watley-McKinney whom I miss dearly. They were all woman of great strength & courage.

Your spirit will never be forgotten.

TABLE OF CONTENTS

Inspirations

Attitude

Closing Poem

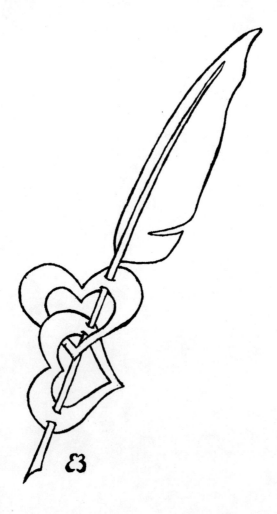

I Choose To Be
In 2003 and even more in 2004

A woman of power that continues to strive

For what I want. To use the wisdom

I've gained from many sources in life.

To put my imagination to the test

To allow my creativity to evolve.

To be more understanding of people and their

Personalities, because no two people are alike.

To put my life in more order than it already is.

To keep the faith

And love I have for Jesus Christ who

Allows me to have the strength and will

To live in this world.

If I

If I share with you my soul
will you take hold,

If I share with you my love
will you thank God for the opportunity,

If I share with you my inspirations
will you share with me the dedication,

If I give you all of me
will you share with me who you are
and what you want to be,

If I give you unconditional love
will you store it or embrace it with the same love,

If I give you my all
could you handle all I have to give,

when I expect the same in return
could you give it in return with no shame.

He Touched Me

As I closed my eyes, I felt his glare
As I closed my eyes I felt his stare
When he touched me for the first time his arms around my
waist,
I could feel my nerves clinch.
My heart skipping a beat, aching with excitement,
As he touched me.
The night grew long with anticipation.
Wanting to feel his caress, soft, strong, long caresses.
As he touched me.
When he touched me for the first time, it was all that I had
imagined.
My body shivered from what he delivered.
His flow was gentle, yet firm. My mind was clear, not one
concern.
Tingling all over, as his hands, lips went lower.
The sensation sooo, you know, you know.
He took me to a place where some have gone and others long to
go.
As he touched me
I knew no fear.
His soft-spoken words were all I could hear.
He poured wine into the mold of my back,
Licked and sipped every drop.
All you could hear was sighing, moaning, don't stop, don't stop.
As he touched me
Lips so soft, saying
Definitely not the last time.

As One

It took great courage to get here
And it will take greater perseverance
To withstand,
But with faith, love and two great
Personalities together
This love affair could endeavor, forever.
As we join from two to one
Let our heart, mind and souls be inseparable.

I've loved you for a long time,
Even before you knew.
Something in me knew that you were the one.
Even through the trying times
When we weren't sure.
You told me my greatest asset was
Perseverance and that I have.

Sometimes through journeys obstacles
try to get in our way,
But faith and commitment is a greater
Power that pushes them aside.
I'll always know that the love I have for you
Will always exceed the need.

Inspired by true love

Going Thru The Motions

We live, we love and we learn.
When you meet someone, get to know someone.
Don't always take their word as their bond
because they might just take you thru the motions.

Pretending and faking is what you might get,
Shaky and uncertainty is what you might get,
Love, care and sharing is what you might get,
Self control and knowledge might be the ultimate.

We live, we love and we learn.
When you meet someone, get to know someone.
Don't always take their word as their bond
because they might just take you thru the motions.
Take your time, try to do what's right,
pay attention, don't be afraid of the height.
Look at what you see, and see what you're looking at.

We all try to climb that ladder
but the end result is what really matters.
We all are looking for love, peace and happiness
but if we don't open our eyes we might be in for a surprise.
Live life to the fullest, you only have one,
open your heart and mind and let it all come.

We live, we love and we learn.
When you meet someone, get to know someone.
Don't always take their word as their bond
because they might just take you thru the motions.

All My Love

All my love, I had for you,
Feelings so strong, sometimes hard to explain.
The feelings of togetherness, feelings you only get from love.
The comfort of sharing till the end of time.
Sitting around thinking of you, how to say I love you
In a different way than the time before.
Sitting in my office, supposed to be instead I
Couldn't think of anything else but you and all my love, I had
for you.

But what did you do. You stored my love
On a shelf like a fiction novel.
You chose to read it only when you felt like it.
Instead of giving back what was given to you.
Taking all my love, I had for you.
Knowing all the time your intentions weren't the same.
Pretending our love was mutual. It couldn't have been:
My love " unconditional", Your love "unconventional".
All my love, I had for you.
A heart so whole you broke in two,
A loving heart you could've destroyed, but stronger than
that I am. To keep striving for the best the unconditional love
I will find.
I'm sure he's out there and he's one of a kind.

Patrice Watley-Hall

You Should Have Loved Me

You should have loved me,
When you had it all, times were good, love was strong.
You had my love, had my devoted attention,
You had a love that was so strong
nothing and no one could come between.
My love for you was real and unconditional,
love that couldn't be explained.
No matter what you did or said
I forgave you and the love never faded.
My love was constant, deliberate, diligent
and consistent.

You should have loved me,
When you had it all, times were good, love was strong.
I will go on to love another
Who will share the kind of love that I have.
I'm not looking for fortune or fame
just unconditional love, true love, no shame.
When dry air moves through the clouds
my mind drifts to you, reminds me of how
I felt during our last days together.
Like dry ice that sticks to your skin and
burns like fire.
Reminds me to never continue to give true love
when you know you're not getting it in return.

Patrice Watley-Hall

Moving On

You phoned me on this particular day
Said you had things to say,
Haven't spoken to you in over a month.
My life is pleasantly calm
shall I listen and allow you
to put my thoughts in a disarray.
You say you have words for me
shall I listen, shall I see
or should I pass and let it be,
What could you possibly have to say
that would make a difference
What could you say that would matter to me.

You've had plenty of opportunity to say
as much as you've wanted,
Your conscious is probably filled with guilt
your mind and thoughts are being taunted.
Well that as it may be, as you can see
moving on with life is where I'll be,
and to you I advise and am making that plea.

You see you've waited until you've lost your way
what words could you possibly have to make me stay.
Miracles do happen in our lifetime,
but with you I can't see it being that kind.

You've had few words and many promises
in the past, but broken promises don't make love last.
There are no more promises that you could make
all I would be inclined to believe is that
they are artificial and fake.

So for your sake, know that anything I've already heard, is about all that I can take.

I guess you need to speak in order to
move on with your life.
I've already spoken to God and he has
already allowed me to move on with mine.
So my advice to you is to do the same
and hopefully you won't continue the stifle
from which you came.
Life and love should not be taken for granted
so in your move on I wish you peace,
and I hope you learned a lesson, so that your
future life will be filled
with joy, and forever more enchanting.

Compliments of Christy Farr Vaughn

Love Can Last Forever...

Love is the most fulfilling emotion.
It allows you to share life with someone
It allows you to speak your inner most feelings
To someone who understands you.
It allows you to share life's experiences
It allows you to feel warmth,
A wholeness that avoids loneliness.

Love can last forever...
Love allows you to feel complete,
Like nothing else you'll ever feel in your
Mind or body.
It allows you to be happy with yourself
It allows you to have compassion in your heart.

Love can last forever...
It allows you to become one soul with another
It allows you to reach a higher level you
Never thought possible.
Love allows you to trust with your eyes closed
And your heart open.
Love gives you an incredible balance
That allows you to have the highest spirit.
If you commit to love
Love can last forever...
And we all long for it.

When You Love Someone

When you love someone whole-heartedly,
And you don't get it in return,
It takes you apart and confuses your soul and heart.

When you love someone and you're spinning
and yearning, heart aching like a burning fire.
When you love someone you don't leave them out in the rain,
to figure out what you want when you don't talk or explain.
A heart so cold it cuts like a knife,
What about the plans to be husband and wife.

When you love someone, don't lead them astray,
Be true and honest with yourself anyway.
A loving heart only wanting to be close,
helps you to strive to be the best
and achieve the utmost.
Life is full of love and love is full of life,
don't stifle yourself have plenty of might.
Life is too short to let it pass us by.
Day in and day out we're put to the test,
But you can't give up, keep looking for the best.

When you love someone, you're honest and open
to create a bond that can't be broken.

Love is the most fulfilling emotion ever,
You can't be afraid of it, try to keep it forever.

Remembering Love

When you've met someone new
that's more down to earth than you
Who knows what he wants
for the most part
He wants to be loved
and to be loved, so do you
You're reaching for each others love
but the distance is between
You long to be near
wishing the other were here
Remembering each others touch
closing your eyes, imagining it again
Pretending to feel the touch
longing to hold each other once again
The joy of pleasing the other
pleasure you can't get from another
Pleasure you had forgotten how to feel
pleasure you imagined would be ideal
The long conversations you share
about the love you long to have
Enjoying each others folding arms
cuddling the other keeping warm
True and unconditional love we seek
a love that's not pretentious but very unique
Remembering how to love and to let love in
remembering it's okay to be in love again.

Time, Happiness & Love

Time is a funny concept
Based on uniformity, but never a constant
You always know that there will be a three o'clock
and a twelve o'clock
but you never know what that hour may bring

Happiness is a funny concept
Everyone searches for it, but rarely is it
ever sustained
What many fail to realize is that anything
so easily created
can be destroyed just as easy.

Love is a funny concept
The tie that binds two together, if one can
find the other to be tied to
It's the breath of life, that everyone says
they can live without
but without that breath, one cannot live.

The **time** is now yours to do what you wish, because I will be your constant, the **happiness** will always be sustained, because everyday we create more. And **love**, because I have found that bond and I am willing to blow that breath of life into you for as long as you will allow.

What Symbols Can't Say

For me only one thing has really been difficult,
putting emotion into words, is that one thing.
For most, that expression is by symbol.
For love, a rose, and for marriage a ring,
but for me a symbol is only symbolic.
Something that takes the place of what you really mean.
To put what I feel into words
is never as easy as it may seem.

"It is only by chance that we happened to meet
And I thank God for the opportunity that he gave me.
For if the clocks were turned backwards and
the event had been changed,
the happiness that has occurred I never would see.
As it goes, love soothes the loneliest souls
and with your love, three fold, the job is done.
Love comes in so many colors, shapes and sizes,
And with some miracle, with you, blended all into one.

Masculine you are, and a mind so strong, a spirit that
shines, and love no greater than your heart and soul.
A combination of qualities that makes your love strong,
and your love, a bond that will make me
as your woman whole."

Believe me when I say, I'm not trying
to scare you, which I know feelings down
on a page will often do.
I'm merely giving you a little taste
of how much I can really love you!

31

When We're Apart

When we're apart
You're still in my heart.
You're always on my mind
You're one of a kind.
Your spirit is so comforting
Like music to my ears
I feel with you I'll be
For many, many years.

When we're apart
I have no fears or worries
You've reassured me and given me courage.
With you my heart has no shield or cover
You have shown me love only for me and no other.

When you feel blue, I do to.
When you're happy and upbeat
I pray these feelings, with me you'll keep.
You inspire me on things I say and can't foresee
It pushes me to strive for what I can be.

When we're apart
We give inspiration so free and true
We keep each other in mind on everything we do.
When we're apart or together you satisfy me
I'm in total comfort knowing you're with me,
Near me, beside me.

With you I speak words that only you understand
Together we see eye to eye, and hand in hand.
I've given you my heart, and you have done the same
With you I feel complete, and ready to take your name.

You !!!

You were kind in just the right measure,
Words that only brought thoughts of
pleasure.
I'm not quick to fall in and out of love,
But with you I gave my heart,
Right from the start.
You were open and honest
A number of things were bad, some
good, some funny.
You weren't afraid to express your feelings
And that quality will surely bring healing.
Of the pain we both have gone through
And together I felt we could conquer
Something new and true.
You seemed too good to be true
You always gave me smiles when I was
blue.
We were many miles apart

But I could see your smile
That gave my days a better start.

You gave me feelings that you could have
denied,
But those feelings you couldn't hide.
I could feel your warm kisses and your
mild side.
We both had our problems
But we gave each other sound advice
On how to solve them.
Me not being accustomed to getting
back what I give,
I was a little hesitant to open up and live.
I could only imagine giving you my all,
Needing to know how you felt
I couldn't make that call.
Afraid to lay my feelings on the line
But could clearly see your feelings
were the same as mine.
My mind not totally sure, my hands
shaking
But still my heart was yours for the taking.

Alone In My Room

Sitting alone in my room
Feeling a little gloom
Spinning the hour glass
Not realizing all the time
That has passed.
While my mind drifted
On thoughts of not wanting to be alone,
Day dreaming about the love I once had
That's still there, but yet gone.
Knowing that we could still be
If only I'd settle for less you see.
Knowing the love is still there,
Knowing we both still care.
Shouldn't be crying
But that's my only outlet,
Feelings of love I'll never regret.
Wanting to change this lonely afternoon
To pleasant one, without gloom.
Knowing that if it were meant to be
It'll come back to me soon.
He wants to make it right
But he's lost in his own sight.
Until he can be a man
I have to take a stand.
Wishing and hoping we find our way
A love bond strong enough to stay.

Patrice Watley-Hall

FIRST ENCOUNTER

Conversation flowing
Emotions growing,
Exploring each other
Touching every base
Just in case, we want to fill
The other ones empty space.
Looking into each others eyes
Storing each moment
In our personal archive.
Small feelings of discomfort
But quickly fading,
Realizing total interest is there
With the life stories we compare
Sharing memories of life
Memories of strife,
Memories we both could put together
To have a better life.
Vibes flowing
Like cool waters running deep
Memories you wanna keep.
The visibility is clear
Of what we both are feeling
Of what we both are hearing,
From the FIRST ENCOUNTER.

Patrice Watley-Hall

I WISH

I wish to have a more fulfilling life,
one filled with love, not heartache and strife.
I wish to have a complete family
one where we sit and eat and not cheat
ourselves of the quality time,
that allows our heart to shine.
I wish to have a life filled with compassion
making my family happy from life's satisfactions.
I wish to have a love so strong
nothing or no one could ever come along
and make things go wrong.
I wish to have an unconditional love
that would clearly be guided by God above.
I wish to have a life of joy, and little pain
one filled with peace, different, very unique
that when you see me smile,
you'll know the joy I'm experiencing I'm giving
someone the same inside.
I wish to have happiness to keep my spirit alive
to keep me humble, to help others strive.
I wish to have a family that will saver the flavor
of what we share, others will want to compare.
I wish to have a world of sunshine
so that when it rains
I don't complain,
but look forward to the next time,
because without sun and rain
I would not see
the rainbows hovering over me.

Reluctant Love

Slowly I melt her icy heart
Like cool waters running deep,
Deep into her heart
To the point where she couldn't pull herself apart,
From the embrace upon her.
She feels me coming
But still doesn't know what touched her.
Soft gentle, yet firm
And mentally challenging.
Slowly embracing the cold
With bold gestures and the
Intellectual conversations
That blew her mind, made her heart shine,
From the glow I instilled.
The ice melting, feeling warm hands
That took a stand to begin
Intoxicating her mind,
With all the love that slipped up from behind.
And the wounds began to heal
From the passion of soft kisses
Feeling the weakness
That made her speechless.
Indulging in the joy
From which she knew nothing of
Truly feeling the warmth of love.

10 Things I Love About You

Your love is genuine
Your sincerity is gentle
Your heart is warm
Your soul is passionate
Your knowledge is powerful
Your voice is strong
Your opinions are bold
Your stability is firm
Your sight sees further than most
And most of all
You love me!

What Would You Do

What would you do if I
massaged your feet
would you be grateful
or take it for granted.

What would you do if I
cooked everyday
would you enjoy without
complaining and offer to
take me out once in a while
or would you complain that
some part of the meal isn't
to your liking.

What would you do if I
greeted you with a kiss each
and every day
would you kiss me back with passion
or turn your head and complain of the
tiring and hard day you've had.

What would you do if I bore
your children
would you cherish us with
unconditional love or would you
leave us to fend for ourselves.

What would you do if I
loved you with tender love and care
would you love me to no end
or would you just............be.

A Mothers Love

There is no love like a mothers love,
No stronger bond on earth...
Like the precious bond that comes from God
A spirit so sweet, mild and unique.

A mothers love is forever strong,
Love spread in just the right measure,
Love you'll forever treasure.

A mothers love forever shines
May God bless all mothers
While on earth and continue
When her days on earth are over
May he lift her up through the gates of heaven.

A mothers love lives on
Through many generations
With God's blessing hand on each one.

Be thankful for our mothers
For they love with a higher love
From the power God has given,
Their love has risen
Above and beyond to an unconditional mothers love.

Who Is She?

She is a devoted Christian
Under no condition
Does she want another position.
She is a mother and grandmother.
A woman of love, strength and courage,
A sister, an aunt.
Never taking things for granted, being nonchalant.
She has contributed a great deal to her
community.
She is a woman of pride and dignity.
She is held by God and his many auxiliaries.
She is loved by many and hated by none.
She has fought many battles
And won them with faith.
Many may try to lead her astray,
But she has God on her side
To pull her his way.

Who Is She?
A woman willing to do
What God wants her to do.
A woman owing no one but God above,
But willing to pay with grace.
A woman moving in the right direction, .
The pathway to heaven.
A woman assertive enough to do what she
believes,
Working hard in any way she can to achieve.
A woman never depending on man
But has all faith in God Almighty
To deliver everything she'll ever need in life.
Who Is She? She is my mother…

I Do – Do You?

I am there for you
Will you be there for me?
I'll lift your spirits when you're down
Will you stand by me, will you stick around.
When times are strained
Will our spirit still twine
Or will it churn, burn and grind

Do you promise not to loose our love
In the mist of life
And loose sight of our ultimate goal
To love, honor and uphold.
Will you hear my cry, my call
Are you really in it for the long haul?
With you I must say
I feeling such a connection
With you as my protection
I know you can't promise me
That you'll do everything right
But promise me you'll always be there
Promise me you'll always sincerely care.

I Do – Do You?

When You Smile

Your smile is radiant
Like no other
It brightens a room
Like there was never any gloom
Existing any where in the air.
Your smile is like a glare
you can compare
to the ray of sun,
a rainbow spun
from the webs of the sky,
feeling the glow high.
Your smile is vibrant
Comforting to the eyes
Looking upon your face
Mellowing another with grace.

From Where Do You Come?

From where to you come
Is it from a dark world?
With no white clouds
Or a world full of sunlight and rainbows?
From where do you come?
Is it from the same path from which I come?
Or are we on totally different pages,
Are we close in comparison or at different life stages?
When you turn the page do you see what I see?
Or do you succumb to be what you think I want you to be.
When you turn the corner
Are you hoping I'm already gone to bed?
Or are you hoping I'm waiting up for you instead?
When you step out bed
Are you excited that we have another day?
Or are you in a hurry to get on with your day.
When you return home
Are you as delighted as I to be in my presence again?
Or are you resorting to that world of pretend.
Whenever, where ever, I hope our hearts
Still beat with the same rhythm.
Because for as long as our hearts beat as one
I'll be sure to know from where you come.

Patrice Watley-Hall

Feeling Passion

From the beginning
I walked though the door
To be welcomed with a hot, steamy bubble bath.
Slightly darkened room
To see the glow of the candles.
You watched me as I undressed
To step into the bath with a look
Of love and admiration
You watched me with eyes
As though to see me for the first time.
My body and mind so relaxed.
Daydreaming of spending all my time with you
Thinking that's all I want to do.
Never loosing touch of
Loving you so much.
Wondering are you feeling
What I'm feeling.
Sensuous and soft
Your fingers lightly touching my skin
Giving a slight sensation
Soft sensual caresses.
Feeligns of excitement
His lips touching my lips
Then pulling back as he teased me.
Sighing wanting to be pleased
By the man of my dreams
Ever so slightly giving me pleasure.

Building A Bridge

Building a bridge of security
that will withstand the weight of time,
building a bridge of security
travelers along the main line,
indurance through the test of time.
Building a bridge of security
Holding together with the strength of a lion,
Built on land as large as Zion.
Building a bridge of security
With passion for people that have passed over
Built to stand tall and strong,
Built to still stand when others have long gone.
Building a bridge of security
Manipulated by many, broken down by none.
With years of pressure caving in
Still holding up the banner for which it stands,
Built strong and sturdy in the land,
With a heart of gold, though strong but soft like sand.
Built to cross the widest sea and deepest ocean,
A soul filled with many emotions.
Building a bridge of security
To withstand and give, when there appears to be
No strength left, she still gives of herself.
Surviving through the cold, the warmth, the rain and
storms. Still standing up tall to live
What a strong and courageous woman she is…

Hope

Hope for peace
Peace within our hearts
Hope for love
Love that's unconditional
Hope for joy
joy that makes your heart melt
Hope for perseverance
Perseverance that is never ending
Hope for strength
Strength to endure all obstacles
Hope to be whole
Whole in heart, soul and mind
Hope for the future
In order to appreciate the past
Hope for God's acceptance
Acceptance into the throne of Heaven.

WOMAN

Women are strong and not to be degraded
many strengths, we are amazing.
We bear our children with the greatest joy
and pride
pick up the pieces, upbeat and alive,
our greatest fears we choose to hide.
Power is knowledge and knowledge is
power
we're eager to achieve and climb the
highest tower.
We are strong when there is no strength
left.
Out hearts are huge, withstand a lot we do
but strong we stand, you know this is true.

We are compassionate and giving
we sometimes fall but we keep on living.
Our lives and our jobs keep us alert
our ups and our downs keeps us down to
earth.

To love unconditionally, yes we know all
about it

We smile when we want to cry
but the strength we have will never die.
We were created to give life and build
and yet some don't feel we're worth the
yield.
We give, we love and we laugh
to soothe our children and our better half.
We strive for the best and we believe
with might and faith we will achieve.
We fight for what we want, we get what
we strive for.
Women are wonders of the world and a
beautiful and
fulfilling life we deserve.

Patrice Watley-Hall

Reflections

Reflections of who I am inside
I won't pretend I'm someone else and hide.
My reflection shows
My heart glistens and glows.

Reflections of who I am inside
Who I really want to be
I work hard at it, this you'll see.

Reflections of who I am inside
I can't hide, my personality
Won't allow it to stay inside.
It oozes from my pores
And shines like the sun.

Reflections of who I am inside
Like the many blessings we receive everyday.
I'm fortunate in every way
Like an aura of the fresh breeze in May.

Reflections of who I am inside
My heart beats loud and strong
The signs I get from above
I can't go wrong,
When I'm pleasantly calm,
It's like soothing melodies from a song.

Reflections of who I am inside
Don't always appear strong and bold,
But when you really open your eyes
It shines like gold,
Rich, vibrant, firm,
Open up your heart and grab hold.

HOLD ON

When something good comes your way
hold on, don't let it get away.
When something good falls in your lap
don't sleep on it, taking cat naps.
When something good slaps you in the face,
don't stand there in a daze, walking at a slow pace.
As you begin to wonder,
the ponder of your thoughts
have lead you astray, for this you may have to pay.

Don't allow negative thoughts
to take control of your mind
you'll soon be left behind,
to deal with the strays,
the stragglers and their own kind,
don't be blind.
Watch out, read between the lines.
For there are several times we don't see the signs.

Don't be blinded by the darkness of night,
open your eyes, most definitely there is a brighter
light.
Hear me, feel me.
Let the positive vibe in side your mind.

God's Miracles

God's creations are a mystery of the mind
We often wonder how and why he's always on time,
but if we keep the faith and keep on believing in him
he will deliver, he will never leave you out on a limb.

If we keep the faith we'll continue to receive
his many blessings, deliverance he does achieve.
God's miracles, he keeps on bringing
God's miracles, let's keep on singing,
about the great blessings we have received
about the many accomplishments we have achieved.

The creator of all things, through our being
he delivers things he has already foreseen
blessings you never before imagined or dreamed of,
but through God's miracles, from heaven above
he is the redeemer.

Through God's miracles he delivers life
he delivers, he delivers us from strife.
He'll lift you up, when darkness falls,
nothing too tough, just pray and give God a call.
Lifting your spirits to new heights
never failing to show you there is a bright light.

The Sound of Laughter

The sound of laughter
children dying of disaster
Praying daily
laying it all in the hands of out master.
The touch of a small hand
in the palm of your own,
for seeing their future
admiring how they have grown.
Feeling great satisfaction
from their wide smiles
and innocent eyes,
their energy and spunk, so alive.
And then the unexpected attack
of life accompanied by crisis,
pain in their faces
you had never imagines possible.
The pain begins
but seems never ending,
hearts breaking, never mending.
Attempting to carry that familiar portrait
that's now less recognized.
Minimizing the simple joys of life
igniting life's strife's.
There serenity, their purity
shines a bright light in a dark world,
in our world of sorrow
they are visions of tomorrow.

Music

Music is water for the soul
drink it up,
it moves you
causing your soul to erupt.
Music is an incision
that heals open wounds
feeling the melodies from every tune.
Music is passion
passion life soft kisses.
Music is listening to the rain
hitting the window pane,
while reminiscing down memory lane.
Music is crucial keys
touched by magical hands,
it's love, love of base, drums and tenor
and every instrumental.

Music soothes the soul
it releases your mind
reaching, grabbing hold
like you're reaching for gold,
feeling the weakness from songs of love
that make you speechless
putting you in a trance
that's so intoxicating,
like making love
it's so amazing.

Music gets you high on life
so relaxing, you forget life's strife's.
Music is food for the soul
feels as if you're in total control.
Music is attitude
a whole new magnitude.
Music is my calm during the storm
makes your heart melt, feeling warm.
Music can bring the world together
through each and every endeavor,
Music is an expression
that has often taught us a lesson
of patients and unimaginable experiences,
learning not to complain but to sustain
the trials and tribulations
to take action to gain satisfaction.
Music is sitting in the rain
not knowing you're getting wet
soothing, like watching the sun set.
Indulge yourself in music
watch the magic
it's our paradise.

Bubble In My Coke

You're my inspiration
My insulation
You pump me up
To never give up
You push me to higher limits.
When I was tired and wanted
To give in to anxiety
You reminded me of my priorities.
When others need to take a break
They pause to take a smoke
But you're the bubble in my coke!

Your Gift

The life in which you're about to bring into this world,
a beautiful baby girl,
a bundle of joy, a jewel, a pearl.
As husband and wife
cherish this life,
as it is a gift from God above
as sweet and pure as white doves.
In return you will be blessed to receive unconditional love.
The arrival of Grace Vaughn
an amazing bond,
will be filled with unforgettable joy and love.

As you take that first look
into her angel eyes,
uncontrollable emotions to your surprise,
will overcome you
and change your life's patterns
and all that you do.

Steven and Christy Vaughn

From your friend Patrice W. Hall

Patrice Watley-Hall

Photo compliments of Christy Farr Vaughn

Release Me

I have left this world, Release me and let me go
God has other plans for me, better than you know.
Please don't loose sleep over my passing
Rejoice and release me and know that we were
happy when we were in each others company.

You already know how much joy you gave me
And I gave the same.
Thank God for the love we have shared,
So I could go to this better place called heaven.
I promise you I won't be alone.

If you must grieve, grieve for a little while
With the comfort of God.
We will only be apart for a little while,
So cherish the loving memories we
Hold dear and near.

Life will go on and I won't be as far as
You may think. If you need to talk to me,
I will always be listening.
I know you're thinking that may be strange
But don't worry, just feel me with your heart.

Always remember that one day we will
Meet again.
I'll be waiting with my arms open
And my heart warm.
I'll see you when Heavens gates open for you.

Inspired by love and Death

I Miss Her

Feelings of despair, nothing can compare,
when someone dear and near to your heart leaves
you.
It's like a hole in your heart that never mends,
heart wrenching pain that never ends.
When she left me I was lost,
I would have done anything to have her back at any
cost.
A child at age 14 and never experiencing the death
of someone so close.
Looking for signs from up above to tell me
what she would like the most.
I miss riding the bus from Thomasville to
Mechanicsville
anxious, trying to decide do I go out and play or
just chill.
Going to church just across the street,
getting there a little early to assure myself of the
same seat.
Her protecting voice even when I was wrong,
like a soft melody, music from a song.
I was mad with the world
didn't understand how God could take her away
from me.

I was only a little girl.
Didn't understand how people sat around,
ate and laughed during a time like this.
Acting as if she was merely dismissed.
I miss her, there is no other like my grandmother.

The tears flowing and the pain so deep
tried to sleep, my sanity I was trying to keep.
Wanted everyone to leave. No eating, no laughing
during the passing of my grandmother.
Filled my life with joy and laughter,
feelings she gave me, no one else could master.
Wanting her to see my goals and accomplishments,
wishing she were here to say I'm so proud,
hoping she knew just how much she meant.

Trying to find that peace to go on,
knowing she won't be coming back, she's gone.
Taking death so hard, trying to find a way to
continue.
I had to keep in mind, that she was in a place
where God sends you.
I miss her, there's no other like my grandmother.

Inspired by love and death

My Time To Go...

It was my time to go
You may not think the time was right
But God cleared my mind and kept me from the fright
He gave me courage to end painful days and restless nights.

He lifted my spirit ad set me free
Trust me, it was my time to go, you must see.
The sadness you feel, replace it with the times we've shared
Turn your tears to sunshine
And in that rainbow you shall see my face
Full of joy and laughter
Then be re-assured I've lived my life in good character.

The emotional bond we share never ends
And I'll continue to hold your place in my heart
Because the body dies but the soul never parts.
And for every ending there is a new beginning...

Patrice Watley-Hall

War, Pain and Deadly Sacrifice

Battling their peers
Trying to refrain from fear
Soldiers full of courage
To defend their country.
Fighting for rights
Rights even they have no idea about
Issues of world politics.

Weapons of war
Assembled for major destruction
Going through personal turmoil
To be loyal
To a world full of hate
Not willing to join together
Not even for Jesus Christ sake.
Witnessing brutal death
And devastating health.
Raging battle fields
Where opponents will never yield,
To save the lives of their
Women and children, allowing hem to live.
Men and women of war
Taking the risk of returning alive
Or ending up in wars personal archive.
Returning home in a body bag
To be buried beneath their countries flag.

Tears of hurt and pain
The soldiers have to sustain
Heart wrenching pain
The sight of unimaginable death
Impacting so many lives
From the torment of wars destruction.
But in the God has the final word
So regardless of what you've seen or heard
HE IS THE VICTORY!!!

Birthdays

We should cherish the day we were born
We feel, as we get older it's a curse, we're scorn.
We celebrate our birthdays
And wait patiently on the next
Though some of us just want to forget.

We have our first party
Though we don't know what's going on
By the time we reach two
We still don't know what to do.
By the time we're three
We've finally begun to see
What's so great about this day
It's exciting you might say.

We should enjoy the air we're breathing
For he allows us to live through each season.
Our childhood goes faster than we realize
We look back and wish we had lived more
Fulfilling and productive lives.
The next few years, we're just having fun
Parties, outings and fun in the sun.

By the time we're thirty we start to worry
Instead of giving life our all
Relying on mere man to decide our call.
In Christ we should trust
Because he will assure we accomplish what we
must.

Soon our golden days are here with less fear
By then we're wiser and can see things bright
and clear.
We feel our last days have arrived
Instead of thanking God we're still alive.
Before our last days let's keep in mind
We were created by God, we're one of a kind,
Throughout our lives there are all kinds of
signs.
Let's broaden our minds and read between the
lines.
Know that we were given life for a reason
Live life to the fullest and celebrate all of
Life's seasons.

Growing Pains

As a child years pass us by
about our age, we start to lie.
About the years we haven't seen
but eventually we must come clean.
We say we're older because we have no clue
about the trials and tribulations that life takes us through.
We want to be adults when we're young
we don't realize those years we'll soon want to prolong.
While we are children we should cherish those years
because sooner than we know we'll be changing many gears.
So many people don't get the chance to be a child
they clean, they cook, take care of their baby brothers,
doing several adult things, taking the place of their mothers.
Coming home from school, taking care of home
cleaning up the place, putting on another face.
Throughout life there are many growing pains
there are great sites to see and fast changing lanes.
Growing pains make us who we are
we still have a long way to go
we're not finished, not by far.
Growing pains teach us many lessons
we start to tell the truth
and make many confessions.
Throughout life's many blessings
growing pains come in different sessions
Live by what you learn
and learn what you live by
Live through life's growing pains
and learn to appreciate.

Ghetto Life

Growing up in the ghetto, not so bad
learned to appreciate everything I had.
Walking home from school, running from the
dogs
walking home from school, through the graveyard
hall.
Scared as hell, didn't know what to expect
were they cruel and vicious or were they pets.
Passing a house with a man in the window
naked as a jay bird, fondling at us.
Mom called the police to report the damn pervert
so we could be safe, learn something,
do some school work.

People at school didn't believe where I lived,
Thomasville Heights, said prove it, so I did.
Invited them over, said get in, move your ass over
they were shocked as hell, I could see it in their
faces,
the smart one said, get over it, I've seen worse
places.
You don't act or talk like you're from around here
you must be afraid and panicked with fear.

I've seen a lot, heard a lot and been through a lot
but you never give up when you've got the power
I made it through like a true survivor.
Shooting and screaming, you could hear through
the night
ducking and dodging staying away from the fights.
Praying that you don't get caught in the cross fire
walking through the cut, listening to drug dealers
and liars.
Always held my head up, never letting where I had
to live
make me feel any less than the next.
Always knew I would do better
knew I would be smart enough, a real go-getter.
Happiness is what I was trying to reach
hope God guides me to that peace.

Lifetime

In a lifetime we share many dreams,
In a lifetime we pray that things are
what they seem.
Life is full of obstacles that get in our way
we're blessed that God allows us to stay.
In a lifetime we try to live our lives to
it's fullest potential,
in a lifetime we focus on what's essential.
Life is what we build and make of it
we blame others when we fall and fail.
Just try picking up the pieces and getting
back on the scale.
In a lifetime we do several deeds
Some bad, some good
but only to God do we have to answer, so take heed,
Use your mind throughout this lifetime
think before acting and you to could succeed.
When life treats you kind, always keep others in mind.
when you have a kind heart, you shall be rewarded
with God's blessings you will not be disregarded.
In a lifetime we get wiser
in a lifetime the wiser, the higher.
In a lifetime we sometimes weaken and we fail.
but we must pray to God to make us strong,
not weak and frail.
In a lifetime we can accomplish many things
let's live and keep our sanity as human beings.

Live Today

Too many times we put off things that brings us joy
too rigid to break away from out comfortable
atmosphere and routine.
Let's not run from what's destined to be
a part of our lives,
let's be willing to make a change for what
God has put before our eyes.
Life does not wait on us,
so let's take some chances and do what we must.
Life has a way of accelerating, as we get older
the promises we make start to take much longer,
as our days get much shorter.

We should try and take some of life's enthusiasm
and channel it into our minds,
We should pay attention to the signals and the signs,
let us not waste time, sometimes we have to take
a leap and read between the lines.
Life is full of surprises
if we use our brains and on occasion, exercise it.
Let's not let life pass us by
Let's capture all the love and joy
that God has planned and set aside.

Loyalty

What is loyalty?
Can we live up to it?
Loyalty-
Do we give what we receive?
Loyalty-
Let's look into it
Loyalty-
Do we give just enough to get by?
Loyalty-
Do we lie about the loyalty we give?
Loyalty-
Do we sit back, pretend and lie
Loyalty-
Do we hide behind the lives we live?
Loyalty-
Do we really know what it means?
Loyalty-
Or do we use it when it's a benefit
Loyalty-
Is it just a word or do we ever commit

Loyalty-
Do we use it to maneuver and manipulate
Loyalty-
Or is it something we use throughout the
years
Loyalty-
Or are we afraid because of betrayal and
our fears
Loyalty-
It's a beautiful and powerful thing
Loyalty-
Let's try to commit to something
Loyalty-
Let's take a chance
Loyalty-
Let's embrace it, our minds will truly
enhance.

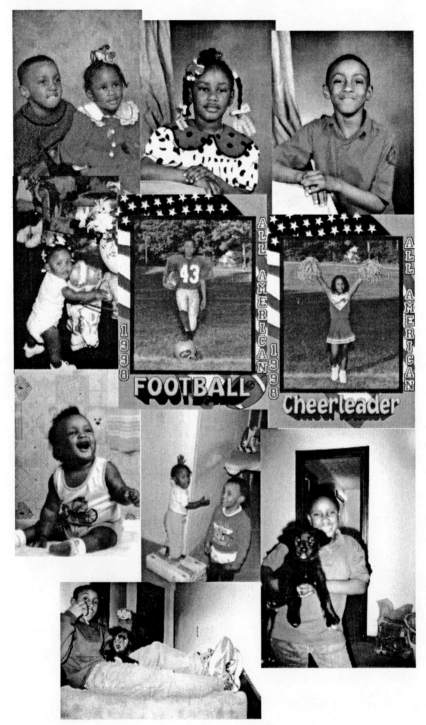

112

Loves of My Life

The loves of my life
Entered this world through my very being
With the miracle of God, foreseeing.
Birth I was able to give
And allow two beautiful children to live.
Not only once, but twice
He allowed me to give life.
When they entered this world
I was filled with joy,
The first love of my life was a baby boy.
Two years later came a little girl,
Both a bundle of love, a jewel, a pearl.
When you give birth, they say you should bond,
But the bond is already there, like a ray of sun.
I looked into their eyes
I could already feel the ties,
That bond parent and child
Pleasantly calm and mild.
Bundles of joy all wrapped in their blankets
Watching them gaze around, looking for familiarity,
Soon to be sure to see you with clarity.
Remembering the pain you thought, unbearable.
Looks of innocence and unconditional love,
A gift of love that you know
Could only have come from God above.

Chances

Sometimes I don't know what road to take,
What choices to make, for other peoples sake.

Being afraid isn't always bad,
But at times can be quit sad.

As long as you face those fears,
knowing God has listening ears.

Unexpected fears come your way,
At that moment, there is nothing
You can say, just pray.

You're sometimes confused about what to do,
But hold on and you'll make it through.

Start thinking with a positive mind,
And you'll be surprised at what you'll find.

Christian Life

We learn early in life, to be Christians
And believe in Christ.
We attend church with our parents, friends,
And congregation.
The program directs us to the order of services
We learn early to listen to the word,
To sit quiet, be still, and take in what we had
heard.
We look up to the pastor
To cleanse our souls for our master.
Some members are hypocritical,
Some visitors analytical,
We sing and we praise in God's grace,
Then we do the unknown, not in God's face.
Little do we know it's all in God's eyes,
For he sees us everywhere, from all sides.

Character

Character is what distinguishes one from
another,
It can stager us or take us further.
Character should be built on firm foundation,
It takes hard work and dedication.
You want to be known for the good character
of your being,
But sometimes that's not what people are
seeing.

We build our character to be it's best,
The world we live in, usually always puts it
to the test.
We try to be strong and keep it at high regards,
We go through ups and downs and it gets hard.
Sometimes we over concern ourselves
With what people think,
But we should live with good standards
And not what we feel will connect us to the
link.

Hear me, Feel me

feel the magnitude
of my attitude
feel my pride
looking at my inner side
we all have dreams
we don't always know
what they mean
try to redeem
what it seems
I do have dreams
that I'm trying to redeem
I am of fire
from what I desire
give me the courage
not to be in a hurry
feel the strength
it's mighty long in length
feel the vibe
of my stride
as I walk
out on the stage
listen to me talk
hear what I say
don't let your mind
wonder and go astray

Small Talk

Person to person
we had this discussion.
You say you're in love
I say you're a scrub.
You say you've been trying
I know you've been lying.
You asked me to stay
I say I don't have time to play.
Look at yourself
it's not good for your health.
You say you're ready for me
you haven't even begun to see.
You have no idea
when you open your eyes
things will become clear.
I'm no around the way girl
in your little world.
So wake up
do a check up.
Put yourself in perspective
then maybe you'll be effective.
Get to know the real me
and just maybe we can be.

Men of Mars

Men of Mars
mysteries of the stars
Men of Mars
are the unknown but reachable beings
that we will forever try to figure out
but to no uncertainty that we ever will
opening their mouths is sometimes an over kill,
but I guess they keep it real,
so we have to find the zeal
in them all, cause
we're usually in it for the long haul.
Like mysteries of the mind
pondering through the brain
gray skies clouding their vision,
impeding their most important mission.
Apprehensive to move forward
all at the same time
wanting, seeking
Relinquishing the opportunity
for unrequited love
staring them in the face
missing their fate.
Allowing their minds to think negative control,
instead of a strong, unconditional love hold.

DECEPTION

Waiting, wanting, longing
Oh there it is
At least you thought that's what appeared
So surreal, but weird,
But that wasn't it
You were tricked again.
But don't sweat it
Because you deserve better
Someone honest that has it together.
It will mend
You thought that was love
But it was the devil in disguise
Who was he thinking of.
He sent someone up
To play with my heart
But guess what
God's going to tear him apart.
The devil thought it was just a myth
He didn't understand
A child of God he was toying with...

Thank You!!!

Thank you for sharing
Thank you for caring,
You've been there when I needed you
no matter what the favor, through and through.
We've had our ups and downs
but somehow manage to turn those frowns into smiles.
I know on occasion I give you a hard time
but you continue to find a way to show me
positive signs,
True friends are hard to find
so let's continue to make one another's
world shine!
You were always kind right from the start,
that's why I'm thanking you from
the bottom of my heart!

to a true friend...

About the Author

Patrice Watley-Hall is a native of Atlanta, Ga., now residing in Lithia Springs, Ga. She attended Draughons College and Fulton High School in Atlanta. She is a single parent of two children and works in the mortgage industry, but her passion is writing. She loves writing poetry and spoken word expressions. Patrice is a woman of love, strength and courage but yet humble. A woman assertive enough to do what she believes. A survivor of many strife's but uplifted by faith. She feels and envisions what she writes. This is her first poetry book but in the near future she plans to publish a second poetry book to include a CD. She also plans to write a novel filled with everyday drama of life, love and the single life. She quotes, "You know, the road to true happiness."

Her accomplishments in poetry are: She is a member of the International Society of Poetry. Since her short time as a member of ISP, she received a plaque for Editors Choice Award and a silver cup trophy for her outstanding achievements in poetry. She is featured in the ISP yearly anthology of poetry & CD entitled The Color of Life and Eternal Portraits.

For more poetry or info.
www.poeticmindvibes.com
&
patrice@poeticmindvibes.com
or by mail
Patrice Watley-Hall
P.O. Box 247
Lithia Springs, Ga. 30122

Printed in the United States
21378LVS00004B/1-99